The First Geologists

William B. Rice

Earth and Space Science Readers: The First Geologists

Publishing Credits

Editorial Director
Dona Herweck Rice

Associate Editor
Joshua BishopRoby

Editor-in-Chief
Sharon Coan, M.S.Ed.

Creative Director
Lee Aucoin

Illustration Manager
Timothy J.Bradley

Publisher
Rachelle Cracchiolo, M.S.Ed

Science Contributor
Sally Ride Science

Science Consultants
Nancy McKeown,
Planetary Geologist
William B. Rice,
Engineering Geologist

Teacher Created Materials
5301 Oceanus Drive
Huntington Beach, CA 92649-1030
http://www.tcmpub.com
ISBN 978-0-7439-0554-1

Table of Contents

Messages from the Past

Earth is a big and interesting place. There's a lot to see and do. There's a lot to figure out, too. One of the great things about Earth is that it can tell us about itself. How? That's simple. Just take a look around, dig, and explore. Earth reveals much about its past, and it can tell us about its future.

Have you ever picked up a rock or fossil and wondered where it came from? For thousands of years, people have wondered the same things. Some of those people did more than just wonder. They worked to figure things out. They were the first **geologists**. They were scientists of the earth.

balancing rock

Tyrannosaurus Rex skull

Ask a Fossil

Fossils are evidence of past life. They are the remains or imprints of living things from long ago. They can be leaf prints, footprints, shell prints, and skeleton prints. The waste from living things can even become fossils!

Fossils are made in different ways. They can be made when a living thing dies and becomes buried by **sediments**, such as ash from a volcano, mud, sand, or **silt**. They can be frozen in ice. They can be mummies, too. Some fossils have been buried in tar for thousands of years.

Most fossils are made when the soft parts of a living thing decay. The hard parts are turned into something like rock. The minerals in the sediments seep into the hard parts of the living thing. They become preserved as fossils. Other fossils are made when the whole living thing is frozen or mummified. Then, the soft parts are included, too.

Fossils are more likely to be made when a living thing dies near a body of water than on dry land. Near water, it is likely to be quickly buried. Over thousands of years, the sediments settle into layers that become **sedimentary** rock. Fossils are often found in sedimentary rock.

Early Geologists

Scientists have been studying Earth for almost as long as people have been living on it. Some of the first geologists came from ancient Greece and Egypt. They learned some of the basics of **geology**. They discovered that fossils were the remains of animals and plants that lived long ago. They found that water deposits sand and silt, and these deposits change the land and water flow.

fossil of an ancient cephalopod

map of ancient Greece

They even figured out the size of Earth itself! This was long before there were maps, compasses, computers, and airplanes to help with that kind of work.

map of ancient Egypt

Eratosthenes

Eratosthenes lived and studied in Egypt. He wanted to figure out the size of the earth. So, he measured shadows at noon in two places. In this way, he found that the distance around the earth was 40,000 kilometers (about 24,800 miles). He was very close to the truth.

Pythias of Assos

Pythias was Aristotle's wife. Aristotle is one of the most famous thinkers and scientists from ancient times. Pythias was also a fellow scientist. Together they studied plants and animals. They even put together an encyclopedia about them. Sadly, women during that time did not often get credit for their work. Poor Pythias! Even Aristotle saw her as only his assistant.

Nicolas Steno

Later in China around A.D. 1000, scientists studied how land was formed. They figured that land must change over time. They began to understand **erosion**. Erosion wears away mountains, rocks, and other landforms.

In Europe about 500 years later, scientists added to this knowledge. They believed that **particles** carried by rivers to the sea would turn into rock over time. They also thought the rock would be **uplifted** to form mountains. They figured that the deposits left in rivers must be thousands of years old. This made them realize that Earth must be many times older.

A short time later, scientists learned something more. It had to do with layers in the earth. The layers are called **strata**. A scientist from Denmark named Nicholas Steno developed several basic rules about them. Three were the most important.

The first rule is that the lowest strata are the oldest because they are laid down first. Strata get younger the higher up they go. The second rule states that when strata are laid down, they spread out from side to side, like a blanket on a bed. Finally, the third law states that underground strata will keep going side to side until they are blocked. These rules may seem simple, but they remain important today. Geologists still use them when they study Earth.

Modern Geology

The study of the earth moved forward, but slowly. That all started to change in the late 1700s. That is when Earth science became its own area of study, and the word "geology" was first used.

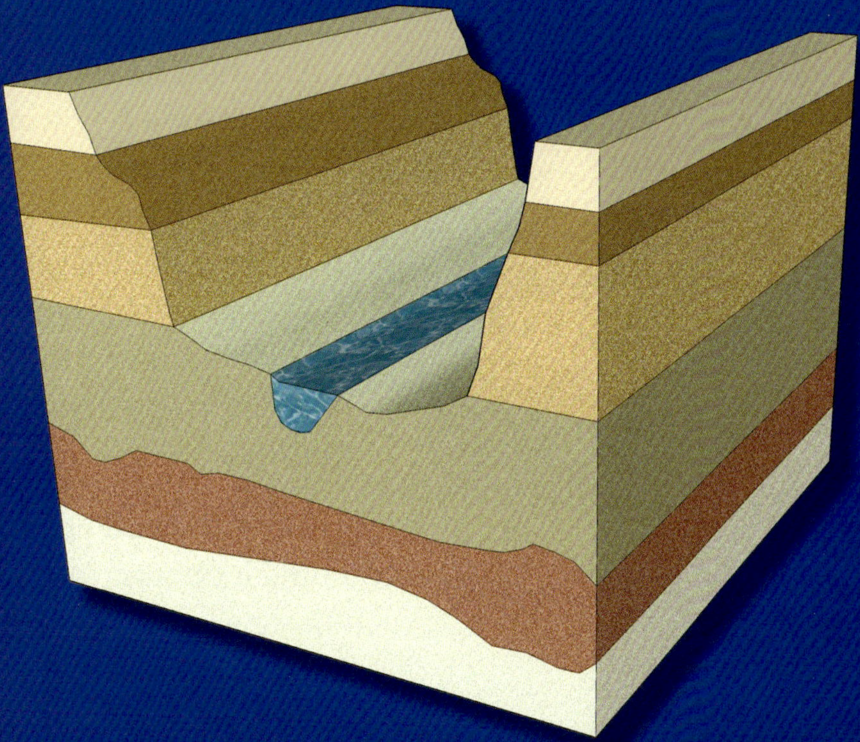

This diagram shows how moving water erodes layers of strata over time, such as in the Grand Canyon.

This image shows the strata at the base of the Colorado River that forms the Grand Canyon.

Oldest Rock

The oldest known rock from Earth is 4.4 billion years old.

James Hutton (1726–1797)

James Hutton

James Hutton was born in Scotland. As a boy, he loved science. In those days, the work a boy would do as a man was often chosen for him. Hutton became an apprentice to a lawyer. An apprentice is someone who is trained to do a job by someone who is experienced in that job. Luckily for Hutton, his employer realized that law wasn't what Hutton wanted. He let Hutton leave to study science.

Hutton studied chemistry with the idea of becoming a doctor. At that time, there was no such thing as geology. He finished his studies and became a doctor. When he could not find work, luck was with him again. He inherited a small farm. That would change his life.

On the farm and in his travels, Hutton began to study Earth's surface. He worked hard to make his farm successful. When it was successful enough, he began to spend nearly all his time studying the land and rocks around him.

Family Life

Hutton never married. He lived on his farm with his three sisters.

Witch!

Martine de Bertereau du Chatlet studied geology in the 1600s. Geology was a new science then. She tried many different things to see if they worked. She tried alchemy, trying to turn metals into gold. She tried dowsing, finding underground water and minerals with twitching sticks. Some people were suspicious of her work. They thought she was practicing magic. She was put to death for being a witch in 1642.

Hutton had questions about what he saw. How did the land come to be this way? How old were the rocks? What formed them? He knew there had to be answers to his questions.

However, it wasn't always easy to find the answers. He couldn't turn to books because there wasn't much written about the earth. He couldn't turn to other scientists because very few were studying the earth. He had to figure things out for himself. He did this mainly through observing and thinking. In this way, he was able to come up with many answers, and he was often right. He thought that forces inside Earth caused by heat could raise mountains. He also thought that the forces of nature had an effect on

Hutton's Unconformity at Siccar Point in Scotland is shown in the photo above. An underground unconformity is shown in the diagram.

mountains, including water deposits, volcanoes, and more. He believed this had been happening for millions of years.

Many people did not agree with Hutton. His ideas went against the common beliefs. But this did not stop him. His ideas explained much of what people saw on Earth. Hutton's new ideas soon replaced the old ones. In time, he wrote a book called *The Theory of the Earth*. This book became the basis for modern geology. He is responsible for the rule that states, "The present is the key to the past." In his own words, James Hutton said, "The past history of our globe must be explained by what can be seen to be happening now." Hutton figured out so much that his book is over two thousand pages long!

Catastrophe!

In Hutton's time, **catastrophism** was the main belief. It says that Earth was shaped through major catastrophes. They were terrible disasters like floods and fires. Many scientists believed that this was true. Hutton didn't agree with them.

William Smith (1769–1839)

William Smith

William Smith lived in England. His father was a farmer. Many thought he would be a farmer, too. He had different ideas. He learned to be a **land surveyor** instead. A land surveyor figures out the lay of the land, on and below the surface.

When Smith was young, he loved to find fossils. He spent a great deal of time looking for them. He studied them, too. From where did they come? He wanted to know more than the scientists of the time could tell him.

Smith himself didn't have much education, but he had a big desire to learn. He figured things out for himself.

In his work as a surveyor, Smith traveled all over England. He was hired to find layers of coal. Coal was and is an important source of heat.

Smith also helped to build canals to move the coal to cities. He surveyed the canal routes. It was a big job that lasted six years. The job made it necessary for Smith to really know about the rocks that were along the routes and canals. He spent a lot of time studying them. He became an expert.

Barges on canals carried coal all over England.

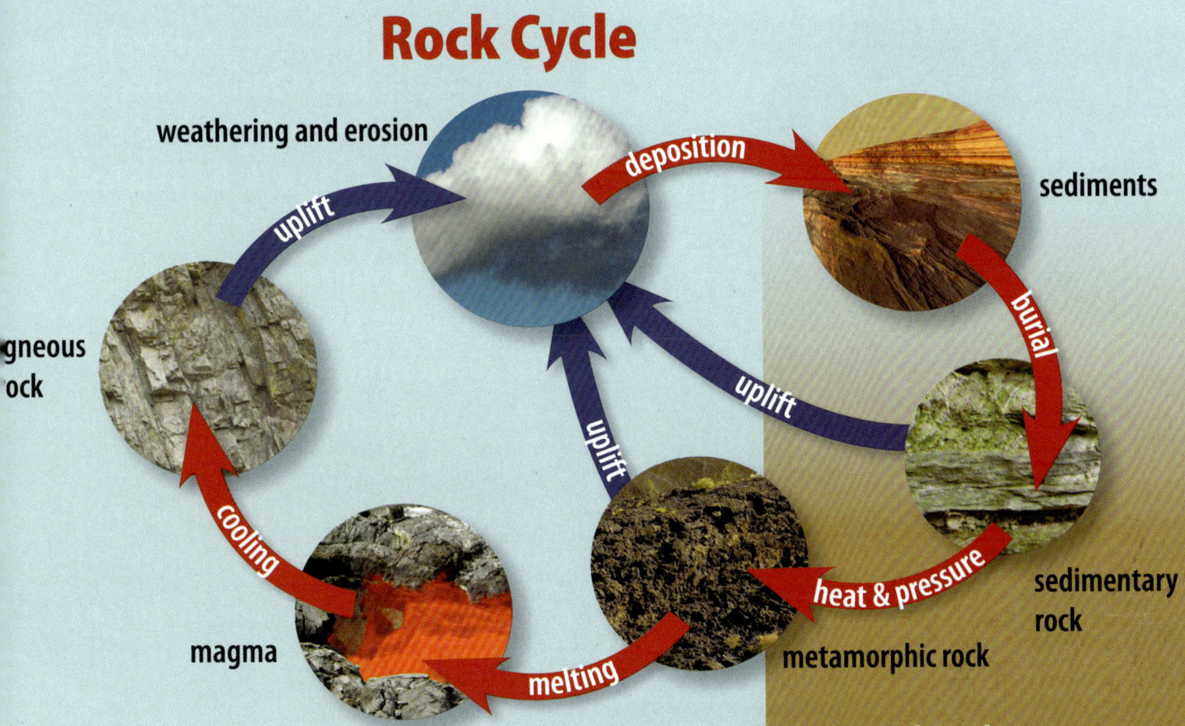

As he worked, Smith found many of the same kinds of fossils all over England. They were in the layers of sedimentary rock he saw. They were also in the same order, from the bottom to the top. This was evidence, he realized, that each layer of coal was a different age. The fossils also said something about when different things lived.

Types of Rocks

There are three rock types: **igneous**, sedimentary, and **metamorphic**. These groups tell about the different conditions under which rocks are made. Igneous rocks form from Earth materials that have melted to liquid **magma**. Magma usually forms deep beneath Earth's surface where it is very hot. When magma cools, igneous rocks are formed. Rocks made by layers of sediment stacked together over time are called sedimentary. Rocks that are changed by pressure and heat are called metamorphic.

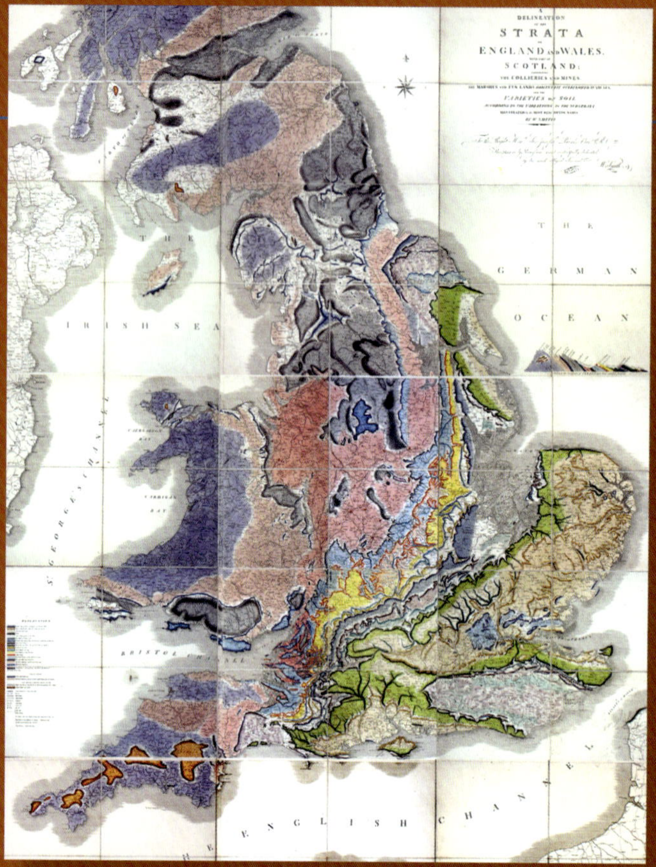

Smith's map

Over the years, he put a lot of what he learned into maps that he made. When his job on the canal ended, he started a big map-making project. He wanted to make a map that showed the geology of all of England and Wales. It was slow work, and he didn't have much money to do it. Finally, he was able to find 400 people who invested in his project. He began the map in 1812. In 1815, it was complete.

Smith's map has been claimed as the first true geologic map. His efforts also set a standard in mapping. Many of the ways Smith noted things on maps are still used today.

When it was first published, the map didn't have a lot of success. Because Smith wasn't well-educated, many scientists didn't think his work could be good. Finally, they realized its value. In 1831, the Geological Society of London created the Wollaston Medal. It is its highest honor. William Smith was given the first one for his big achievement.

Wollaston Medal

Mary Anning

Mary Anning (1799–1847)

Mary Anning is important because she was one of the very first **paleontologists**. She grew up in the coastal town of Lyme, England. Lyme is known for its beautiful cliffs. These cliffs are filled with fossils. Mary's father taught her how to collect them. In 1810, Mary's father died. Mary and her mother started a business of collecting and selling fossils. They sold their fossils to museums. This had a bad effect on credits given to Mary for her finds. Why? Museums gave credit when fossils were given as a gift to them, not when they had to buy them. Thankfully, Mary was given credit for locating the fossils of *Ichthyosaurus* and *Plesiosaurus*, two types of dinosaurs.

Plesiosaurus fossil

Ichthyosaurus fossil

Friedrich Mohs (1773–1839)

Friedrich Mohs

The study of minerals was popular long before the study of geology was. Minerals are naturally occurring substances that Earth makes. They form **crystals** and are made of certain chemicals. Many people confuse them with rocks.

Friedrich Mohs was a German **mineralogist**. He studied minerals. Mineral collecting was very popular at the time. Some minerals such as diamonds are very valuable.

A rich banker hired Mohs to identify his minerals for him. Mohs had to find ways to do it. He knew a great deal about minerals from his studies and in his work in a mine. He had spent a lot of time looking at and studying minerals of all kinds. But he knew there had to be a better way to identify minerals than just by looking at them.

salt mine

Importance of Minerals

Minerals are important because they are used to make many things people need. Some minerals are used to make buildings, windows, and electronic equipment. Some are used to make jewelry. Even the human body needs minerals to survive. We get many important minerals by eating good food and by taking vitamins.

He saw that each mineral had a different level of hardness. The way to test hardness is through a scratch test. Mohs developed a hardness scale. The scale ranged in numbers from one to ten. For example, the mineral talc is very soft. This is because every other mineral can scratch it. So, Mohs gave it the hardness level of one. A diamond on the other hand is very hard. No other mineral can scratch it. Mohs gave it the hardness level of ten. These two minerals set the two extremes for the hardness scale. All other minerals fall between these two extremes.

Today, the **Mohs Hardness Scale** is a guide used by every geologist.

Mohs Hardness Scale

Number	Mineral
10	diamond
9	corundum
8	topaz
7	quartz
6	feldspar
5	apatite
4	fluorite
3	calcite
2	gypsum
1	talc

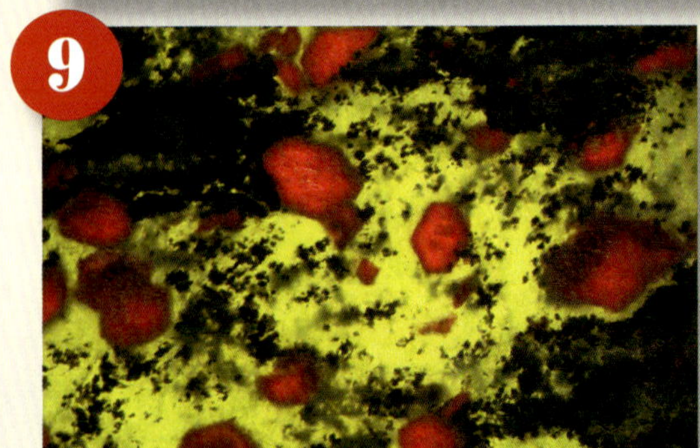

8

7

6

5

4

3

2

1

Alfred Wegener (1880–1930)

Alfred Wegener

Alfred Wegener was a German scientist. He saw the close fit between the coasts of Africa and South America. He thought the continents looked like puzzle pieces that were pulled apart. Fossils from the two continents were often similar. How could this be when a large ocean now divided the two? Wegener thought the land must have been joined at one time. He believed that through earth activity, they had drifted apart. He called this activity **continental drift**. This was a new theory at the time. Many scientists disagreed with him. They believed that the continents were once joined by a section of land that was now under the ocean. But Wegener stood by his theory. He wrote a book about his ideas. Alfred Wegener's ideas help us to understand earthquakes, volcanoes, mountains, and more.

Charles Lyell

Charles Lyell (1779–1875) loved to study geology. He wrote many books on the subject. His first book, *Principles of Geology*, led to the wide acceptance of James Hutton's ideas. Lyell's book *Elements of Geology* spread new ideas about geology to the world. He also made an important discovery about fossils and rock layers. He realized that by counting the number and types of fossils, people can understand the ages of some rocks.

Tools of Geology

Think geology sounds like fun? First, you'll need to load up your kit bag. Here are a few things geologists use when out in the field looking at rocks.

- A **Brunton compass** is used to figure out the angle that rocks are leaning and their direction.
- A hand lens is a small magnifying glass. It's used for looking at rocks up close.
- A notebook and pencil are used for writing what is seen.
- A field map is used to record points so they can be found again.
- A tape measure is used to measure things in the field.
- A rock hammer is used to break open rocks and to pry them from the ground.
- An acid bottle with weak acid is used to test chemicals in rocks.
- An altimeter is used to figure out your height above sea level.
- A GPS receiver is used to figure out where you and the rocks are.

Florence Bascom (1862–1945)

Florence Bascom was born in Massachusetts. Bascom first learned about geology during a trip when she was young. She went with her father and his friend. The friend taught geology. Her interest was sparked, and she wanted to learn more. The problem was that Bascom lived during a time when many women did not go to college or study science. That didn't stop Bascom! She went to college and dealt with the troubles of being a woman in a man's world. For instance, when she was a student at Johns Hopkins University, she had to sit behind a screen during some classes. This was so she wouldn't bother the young men!

Bascom eventually earned a Ph.D. from Johns Hopkins University. She then became one of the first female geologists. She had an understanding of mountains and how they are formed. During her lifetime, Bascom was listed as one of the top one hundred geologists in the world. Impressed? She was also the only woman on the list! Today, thousands of women around the world are skilled geologists.

Winifred Goldring (1888–1971)

Winifred Goldring was born in Kenwood, New York. She grew up in a time when many women did not study science. Goldring not only studied science, but she also eventually taught it. She especially loved geology and fossils. In an effort to share her love of the earth and all its treasures, she wrote a book called *The Handbook of Paleontology for Beginners and Amateurs*. It was published in 1929. It made many people aware of fossils and the study of them. It was also often used to teach students in colleges.

Geophysicist: Joann Stock

California Institute of Technology

Explore More

Joann Stock is fascinated with Earth and earthquakes. She has worked in many places around the world. She has even gone on TV to tell people how to be safe when an earthquake happens.

Stock's interest in geology began in college. A professor took her on an expedition to Greece. "I just thought it was really fun to do research.

How Do They Know?

What's on the ocean floor? Scientists can figure out what it looks like by using boats with special tools. They can also go down in a submarine and see it with their own eyes.

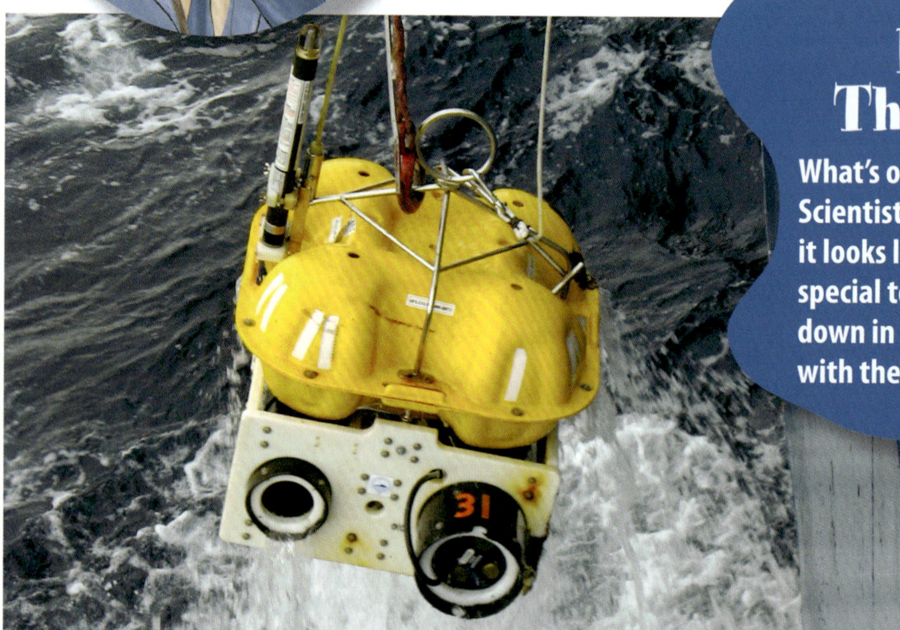

Seismographs record vibrations in the ground—even under the sea!

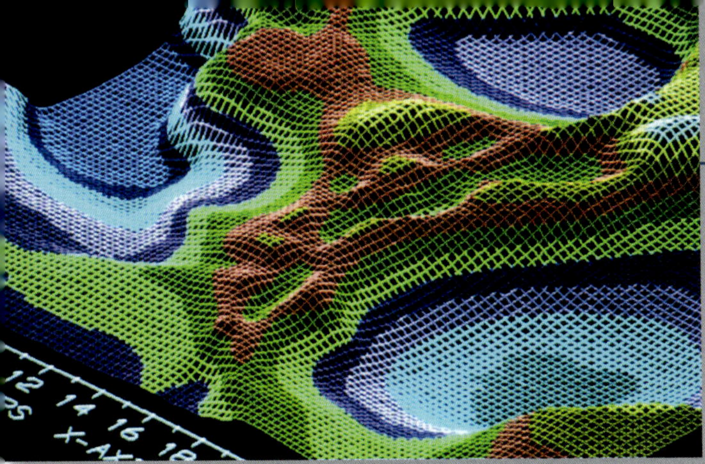

Sometimes underground forces push molten rock to the surface, as in volcanic eruptions.

Being There

If you were a **geophysicist** you would study the structure of Earth and how it changes. You might . . .

- measure glaciers.
- look for oil or coal.
- find safe places to put bridges.

I liked learning things that nobody knew before," Stock tells Sally Ride Science.

Maybe that is why Stock is interested in exploring the ocean floor. Most of it has not been explored. Did you know that some earthquakes start there? Stock studies those earthquakes. It is not easy to study the ocean floor—it is covered with tons of water. So, Stock says there are still a lot of mysteries down there. Where there is a mystery, that is where you will find Joann Stock.

Did You Know?

Earthquakes are caused by plate tectonics, the movement of pieces of Earth's surface.

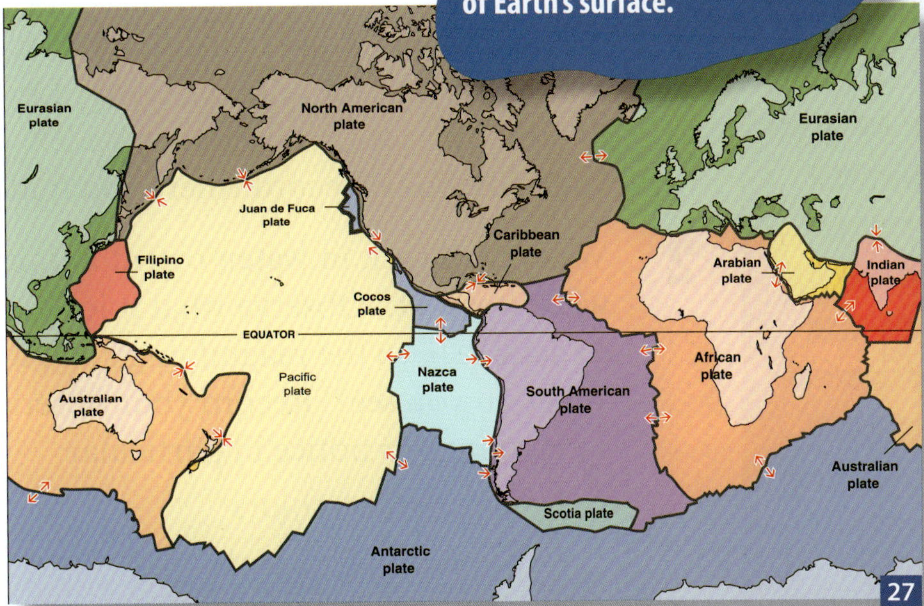

Lab: Observing to Learn about Rocks

You can learn a great deal about rocks just by looking at them. Follow these steps to see what you can learn.

Materials

- five different rocks
- water
- magnifying glass
- notebook
- pen or pencil

Procedure

1. You will need to find five different rocks in nature. It is important that they are different. Look around outside in different places. Find them in widely different areas. In your notebook, record where you find each one.

2. Wash each rock in water, one at a time. Look at each rock when it is wet. Observe what it looks like. Pay attention to details. Use the magnifying glass to help you see better. What do you see? Record your observations. Here are some things to notice in particular:
   - the color or colors
   - presence of crystals

- size and shape of crystals or particles
- shininess of crystals or particles
- amount of one kind of crystal or particle compared to others

3 Look again at each rock when dry. Pay attention to the details again. What do you see? Record your observations. Use the same list as above.

4 Where did you find each rock? What does its location tell you about the rock? Did you find it in a stream bed? Was it on a mountain or in a valley? Was it in a field, by a lake, or at the ocean? Was there anything important near where you found the rock that might have affected it?

Conclusion

Geologists ask themselves many questions when studying the earth and rocks. In order for you to learn about and identify rocks, you'll want to ask lots of questions like the ones listed above. If you want to study rocks even further, you can also test them for hardness or conduct chemical testing. You will need special tools and a lab for these sorts of tests. With the right tools and the right teacher, you can learn many things about the world of rocks and minerals.

Glossary

Brunton compass—a device used to figure the angle of rocks and their direction

catastrophism—the belief that major changes in the earth's crust result from catastrophes rather than gradual processes

continental drift—the movement, formation, or re-formation of continents (as described by plate tectonics)

crystals—a solid formed by a chemical with a highly regular atomic structure

erosion—condition in which the earth's surface is worn away by the action of water, wind, and air

fossil—any evidence of former prehistoric life

geologist—a person who studies geology

geology—the study of rocks and other substances that make up the earth's surface

geophysicist—a geologist that uses physical principles to study the properties of the earth

igneous—a type of rock formed by cooled magma

land surveyor—a person who determines points and lines of direction on the earth's surface

magma—molten rock in the earth's interior

metamorphic—rocks that are changed by heat and pressure

mineralogist—someone who studies minerals

Mohs Hardness Scale—a scale for classifying minerals based on relative hardness, determined by the ability of harder minerals to scratch softer ones

paleontologist—someone who studies fossils

particle—an extremely small piece of matter

sediment—particles that can be transported by fluid flow

sedimentary—made from sediment left by the action of water, ice, or wind

silt—a sedimentary material consisting of very fine particles intermediate in size between salt and clay

stratum (strata)—a horizontal layer of rock, earth, or similar material

uplift—to raise or elevate

Index

Sally Ride Science

Sally Ride Science™ is an innovative content company dedicated to fueling young people's interests in science. Our publications and programs provide opportunities for students and teachers to explore the captivating world of science—from astrobiology to zoology. We bring science to life and show young people that science is creative, collaborative, fascinating, and fun.

Image Credits

Cover: Bychkov Kirill Alexandrovich/Shutterstock; p.3 Jason Bodine; p.4 (top) Jason Vandehey/Shutterstock; p.4 (bottom) Kanwarjit Singh Boparai/Shutterstock; p.4–5 Bob Ainsworth/Shutterstock; p.5 (top to bottom) Falk Kienas/Shutterstock; Paul Maguire/Shutterstock; Photos.com; Jason Vandehey/Shutterstock; p.6 Mitja Kosir/Shutterstock; p.6 (left) Diego Barucco/Shutterstcok; p.6 (right) Photos.com; p.7 Photos.com; p.8 The Granger Collection, New York; p.9 (top) Tim Bradley; p.9 (bottom) Photos.com; p.10 (top) North Wind Picture Archives/Alamy; p.10 Cynthia Kidwell/Shutterstock; p.11 The Granger Collection, New York; p.12 (top) Photos.com; p.12 (bottom) Tim Bradley; p.13 Jim Sugar/CORBIS; p.14 (top) The Granger Collection, New York; p.14 (bottom) Hulton-Deutsch Collection/CORBIS; p.15 (clockwise from top left) Sally Wallis/Shutterstcok; Jan Kaliciak/Shutterstock; BONNIE WATTON/Shutterstock; Robert O. Brown Photography/Shutterstock; Jan Kaliciak/Shutterstock; Brian Wathen/Shutterstock; p.16 Tim Bradley; p.16 (bottom) Tim Bradley; p.17 (background) Peter Elvidge/Shutterstock; p.17 (top) SPL/Photo Researchers, Inc.; p.17 (right) Biophoto Associates/Photo Researchers, Inc.; p.17 (bottom) Lawrence Lawry/Photo Researchers, Inc; p.18 (top) Rick Reason; p.18 (bottom) Puchan/Shutterstock; p.19 (top) Kasia/Shutterstock; p.19 (bottom) Natalia V. Guseva/Shutterstock; p.20 (#10) Ivan Stevanovic/Shutterstock; p.20 (#9) Michael Pettigrew/Shutterstock; p.21 (#8) Dawn Hagan/iStockphoto; p.21 (#7) Koval/Shutterstock; p.21 (#6) Mark Rasmussen/Dreamstime.com; p.21 (#5) GC Minerals/Alamy; p.21 (#4) Randall Stewart/Shutterstock; p.21 (#3) Phil Kestell/Shutterstock; p.21 (#2) Alexander Maksimov/Dreamstime.com; p.21 (#1) Graca Victoria/Shutterstock; p.22 (top) The Granger Collection, New York.; p.22 (bottom) North Wind Picture Archives/Alamy; p.23 (background) Kavram/Shutterstock; p.23 Rick Reason; p.23 (bottom) Jason Bodine; p.24 (top) Rick Reason; p.24–25 Greg Randles/Shutterstock; p.25 Rick Reason; p.26 (top) Tim Bradley; p.26 (bottom) NSF Ridge 2000 Research Program; p.27 (top) Albert E. Theberg/NOAA; p.27 (bottom) Tim Bradley; p.28 (top) Paul Maguire/Shutterstock; p.28–29 Nicoll Rager Fuller; p.32 Getty Images